Little John Boy Who Dreamed Big

A Motivational, Inspirational, and Heartwarming Book for Kids (Ages 6-9)

ARTER

Copyright © 2024 by A. Arter. All rights reserved. No part of this publication may be reproduced, distributed, or transmitted in any form or by any means, including photocopying, recording, or other electronic or mechanical methods, without the prior permission of the publisher, except for brief quotations incorporated in reviews and other non-commercial uses permitted by copyright law.

Chapter 1: A Little Boy with Big Dreams

In the small, peaceful town of West Newbury, there was a bright and cheerful boy named John Cena. John had big blue eyes that sparkled with excitement and a head full of messy blonde hair that always seemed to be in a hurry to grow. He loved spending his days playing outside, running with his friends, and exploring the world around him.

One of John's favorite things to do was watch wrestling on TV. On Saturday mornings, after a delicious breakfast of pancakes and syrup, John would settle down in his cozy living room. His parents would turn on the TV, and John's eyes would grow wide as he saw colorful wrestlers jumping and flipping in the ring.

These wrestlers were larger than life. They wore flashy costumes, performed incredible stunts, and moved with amazing strength and speed. To John, they were like superheroes who could do anything. He admired their bravery and how they always fought for what was right.

One Saturday, after watching an exciting wrestling match where the hero defeated the villain and was lifted up by the cheering crowd, John turned to his family with a big smile on his face. "I want to be a wrestler when I grow up!" he declared, his voice full of enthusiasm. "I want to be strong and brave, just like them!"

His parents exchanged knowing glances and then smiled warmly at him. "John, that's a wonderful dream," his mom said. "But remember, achieving big dreams takes a lot of hard work and dedication."

John nodded eagerly. "I know, Mom! I'm ready to work hard every day to make my dream come true." He felt a sense of excitement and determination bubbling inside him. Even though he was just a little boy, he was ready to start working towards his big goal.

Chapter 2: Hard Work Begins at Home

John's parents were incredibly supportive of his dream. They wanted to help him reach his goals, so they decided to turn their garage into a small home gym. They set up weights, exercise mats, and even a punching bag. John was thrilled when he saw the transformation. It felt like his very own wrestling training center!

Every day after school, John would rush home, eager to begin his workout. His dad would be waiting for him, ready to guide him through the exercises. "Okay, John, today we're going to start with some basic strength training," his dad said, showing him how to lift small weights. "Remember, it's important to use the right technique so you don't hurt yourself."

John listened carefully and followed his dad's instructions. At first, lifting the weights was tough. His arms felt sore, and he was out of breath quickly. But John was determined to push through. He imagined himself as a wrestler, lifting heavy weights and performing amazing moves. "I'm getting stronger every day," he told himself.

As weeks turned into months, John's muscles grew stronger, and his workouts became a part of his daily routine. He would wake up early to exercise before school and would train again after finishing his homework.

John learned to enjoy the challenge, and he loved seeing his progress. Each time he finished a workout, he felt a sense of accomplishment and pride.

One day, John's dad came to the garage with a new set of weights. "You're doing great, John. It's time to start lifting a little more weight," he said. John felt excited and a bit nervous. He had worked hard to get to this point, and now he was ready to take the next step.

Chapter 3: School Days and Facing Challenges

John's dream of becoming a wrestler was always on his mind. He continued to work hard and improve his strength, but he also knew that he needed to be a good student. At school, John paid attention in class, did his homework, and tried to be helpful to his classmates. He believed that being a great wrestler meant being a great person too.

John loved sharing his dream with his friends. During lunch, he would excitedly tell them about his training and the moves he was learning. "I'm going to be a wrestler someday!" he would say. "I'm practicing really hard!"

Some of John's friends were supportive and cheered him on. But others didn't believe in him. They laughed and said, "Wrestling is just a game. You're just a kid. How can you ever become a real wrestler?"

John felt hurt by their words, but he tried not to let it get him down. He remembered what his parents had taught him about believing in himself. One day, after school, John went home feeling sad. "Mom, some kids don't think I can become a wrestler. They laugh at me," he told her.

His mom hugged him tightly. "John, dreams are special and sometimes people don't understand them. What's important is that you believe in your dream and keep working hard. People might not always support you, but if you stay true to yourself, you can achieve anything."

John felt comforted by his mom's words. He decided that he would continue working hard and stay focused on his dream, no matter what anyone said. Every day, he practiced his wrestling moves, trained his body, and stayed positive.

Chapter 4: Growing Stronger, Inside and Out

As John grew older, he continued to pursue his dream of becoming a wrestler. His training became more serious, but he also knew that being a good person was just as important as being strong.

John joined the school football team to build his strength and agility. Football was exciting and challenging. John loved running on the field, catching passes, and working as a team. It helped him become faster and more coordinated, skills that would be useful in wrestling. Every day, he practiced with his team, improving his skills and learning new techniques.

One day, John's coach noticed how hard he was working. "John, you're doing an amazing job out there," the coach said. "I see a lot of dedication in you. Remember, working hard on the field will help you in everything you do."

John felt proud and motivated. He continued to practice football and work out in the garage, balancing both activities. His muscles grew stronger, and he felt more confident. He started to see the results of his hard work, and it made him even more excited about his dream.

John also learned valuable lessons about teamwork and sportsmanship. He always encouraged his teammates and celebrated their successes. He learned that being a good teammate was just as important as being a good athlete. "We all help each other become better," he would say.

At home, John's family noticed his growth. He was more disciplined, focused, and kind. His parents were proud of how he balanced his training with his schoolwork and how he treated others with respect. "John, you're growing into a wonderful young man," his mom said. "Keep working hard and being kind."

John continued to train diligently. He practiced wrestling moves, lifted weights, and ran laps. He set new goals for himself and worked hard to achieve them. Each day, he felt more prepared and excited about his future as a wrestler.

Chapter 5: The First Wrestling Match

When John turned 15, he heard about a local wrestling competition in his town. The competition was a big deal for him—it was his chance to step into the wrestling ring and test his skills. John was excited and a little nervous, but he knew this was an important step in his journey.

John prepared for the competition by training even harder. He practiced wrestling moves in the garage, visualized himself in the ring, and worked on his fitness. "This is my chance to show everyone what I've been working for," he thought. He wanted to give his best performance and make his dream come true.

On the day of the competition, John arrived at the gym early. He saw wrestlers warming up, stretching, and practicing their moves. The gym was buzzing with energy, and John could feel his excitement growing. He watched the other wrestlers and tried to learn from their techniques.

When it was John's turn to compete, he felt his heart race. He stepped into the ring, and the crowd cheered. John took a deep breath and focused on his training. His opponent was strong and experienced, but John was determined to do his best.

The match was intense. John and his opponent moved quickly, performing flips and holds. John felt his muscles aching, but he remembered all the hard work he had put in. "I can do this," he told himself. "I've trained for this moment."

With every move, John's confidence grew. He used his strength and agility to gain the upper hand. The crowd cheered loudly as John made a final, powerful move and won the match. John's heart soared with joy. He had achieved a big milestone in his journey to becoming a wrestler.

After the match, John's family and friends congratulated him. "You did great, John!" his dad said, giving him a big hug. "We're so proud of you."

John felt a deep sense of pride and accomplishment. Winning the match was a huge achievement, but he knew it was just the beginning. He was more motivated than ever to continue working hard and chasing his dream.

Chapter 6: The Big Opportunity

As John continued to participate in wrestling competitions, his hard work started to pay off. People began to notice his talent and dedication. One day, John received exciting news—he was invited to try out for a professional wrestling league. This was a huge opportunity, and John was thrilled.

John knew that making it to the professional league would be challenging. He wanted to make the most of this chance, so he trained with even more dedication. He practiced his wrestling moves, worked on his strength, and visualized himself succeeding in the tryouts.

Every day, John pushed himself to improve. He lifted heavier weights, ran faster, and practiced his techniques until they were perfect. He also made sure to get plenty of rest and eat healthy foods to keep his body strong and ready.

The day of the tryouts arrived, and John felt a mix of excitement and nerves. The tryouts were being held in a large arena, filled with hopeful wrestlers and coaches. John took a deep breath and reminded himself that he was ready.

John performed his wrestling moves with confidence. He showed the judges his skills, strength, and determination. He gave it his all, knowing that this was his chance to prove himself. John felt proud of his performance, knowing he had worked hard to get to this point.

After the tryouts, John waited anxiously for the results. He spent the time reflecting on his journey and feeling grateful for the opportunity. When the news finally came, it was amazing—John had been accepted into the professional wrestling league!

John was overjoyed. This was a dream come true, and he knew it was the result of all his hard work and dedication. His family celebrated with him, and John felt a deep sense of accomplishment. He was excited to start this new chapter in his journey and eager to continue pursuing his dream.

Chapter 7: Achieving the Dream

Starting his career in the professional wrestling league was an incredible experience for John. The matches were tougher, the competition was fierce, and the training was more demanding. But John was determined to succeed. He continued to work hard, stay focused, and never lose sight of his dream.

John quickly made a name for himself in the wrestling world. He became known for his incredible wrestling skills, his powerful moves, and his positive attitude. Fans admired him not only for his athleticism but also for his kindness and generosity.

John used his fame to inspire others. He participated in charity events, visited children in hospitals, and spoke to young people about following their dreams. He wanted to show them that with hard work and determination, anything was possible.

John's success didn't come without challenges. There were times when he faced tough opponents, dealt with injuries, and felt exhausted. But through it all, John remained focused on his goals. He kept pushing himself, learning from his experiences, and growing as a wrestler.

John also made sure to stay true to himself. He always remembered the values he learned growing up—hard work, kindness, and perseverance. He continued to be a role model for others, showing that being a champion was not just about winning matches but also about being a good person.

As John's career continued to flourish, he never forgot where he came from.

He continued to train hard, stay humble, and support his fans. John's journey from a young boy with a big dream to a successful professional wrestler was a testament to the power of hard work, determination, and a big heart.

John's story inspired many people, proving that with dedication and kindness, you can achieve your dreams and make a positive impact on the world.

Conclusion: You Can Be a Champion Too

So, if you have a dream, no matter how big or small, remember John Cena's story. Work hard, believe in yourself, and always be kind to others. Just like John, you can achieve anything you set your mind to. Keep dreaming, keep working, and never give up. With a big heart and determination, the world is full of amazing possibilities waiting for you to discover.

Made in the USA
Columbia, SC
08 May 2025